Crisis as
Opportunity

The Lessons Learned Series

Learn how the most accomplished leaders from around the globe have tackled their toughest challenges in the Harvard Business Press *Lessons Learned* series.

Concise and engaging, each volume in this series offers fourteen insightful essays by top leaders in industry, the public sector, and academia on the most pressing issues they've faced. The *Lessons Learned* series also offers all of the lessons in their original video format, free bonus videos, and other exclusive features on the 50 Lessons companion Web site www.50lessons.com/crisis.

Both in print and online, *Lessons Learned* contributors share surprisingly personal and insightful anecdotes and offer authoritative and practical advice drawn from their years of hard-won experience.

A crucial resource for today's busy executive, *Lessons Learned* gives you instant access to the wisdom and expertise of the world's most talented leaders.

Other books in this series:

Leading by Example	*Executing for Results*
Managing Change	*Sparking Innovation*
Managing Your Career	*Making Strategy Work*
Managing Conflict	*Doing Business Globally*
Starting a Business	*Going Green*
Hiring and Firing	*Weathering the Storm*
Making the Sale	

Crisis as Opportunity

LES50NS

www.50lessons.com/crisis

Boston, Massachusetts

Printed in the United States of America
13 12 11 10 09   5 4 3 2 1

Library of Congress Cataloging-in-Publication Data

Crisis as opportunity
        p. cm. — (Lessons learned)
    ISBN 978-1-4221-3980-6 (pbk.)
  1.   Entrepreneurship. 2.   Financial crises.
3.   Success in business. I.   Harvard Business
School. Press.
    HB615.C75 2009
    658.4'012—dc22

                              2009014937

⊰ A NOTE FROM THE ⊱ PUBLISHER

In partnership with 50 Lessons, a leading provider of digital media content, Harvard Business Press is pleased to offer *Lessons Learned*, a book series that showcases the trusted voices of the world's most experienced leaders. Through personal storytelling, each book in this series presents the accumulated wisdom of some of the world's best-known experts and offers insights into how these individuals think, approach new challenges, and use hard-won lessons from experience to shape their leadership philosophies. Organized thematically according to the topics at the top of managers' agendas—leadership, change management, entrepreneurship, innovation, and strategy, to name a few—each book draws from 50 Lessons' extensive video library of interviews with CEOs and other thought leaders. Here, the world's leading senior

A Note from the Publisher

executives, academics, and business thinkers speak directly and candidly about their triumphs and defeats. Taken together, these powerful stories offer the advice you'll need to take on tomorrow's challenges.

As you read this book, we encourage you to visit www.50lessons.com/crisis to view videos of these lessons as well as additional bonus material on this topic. You'll find not only new ways of looking at the world, but also the tried-and-true advice you need to illuminate the path forward.

⇥ CONTENTS ⇤

Contents

Contents

If you could eliminate doubt and move boldly ahead with confidence knowing that you were facing the best opportunity of your lifetime, would you do it?

That is exactly how the world's best business leaders see the crisis unfolding in today's wildly turbulent environment. In this book, successful leaders will share with you firsthand accounts of disaster they averted while competitors stood paralyzed with fear. You will learn how the world's most successful CEOs *mine* every ounce of adversity for hidden assets and insights they can use to their strategic advantage.

This book is packed with counterintuitive intelligence from executives who have seen it all. You will get their practical advice based on the hard lessons they learned as their industries raced to transform themselves. They're gaining market share because of, not despite, the changes their customers are demanding in this time of epic turmoil. As the world is bursting apart, new models have emerged that are providing the chance of a lifetime to find the best in your people and get closer to your clients than ever before.

You'll hear how Marriott embraced customers and boosted market share by viewing the tough economy as an extraordinary opportunity to pick up assets at bargain prices. As the famed Ritz-Carlton franchise teetered on bankruptcy, J. W. Marriott Jr. swooped down to buy it. "We constantly have radar going 'round like on a ship," the Chairman and CEO of Marriott International says. When a great brand gets cheap, "we're there to get it."

Ikea also profited from planning for the worst. "If you have an offensive strategy in a downturn, like we have, it is an opportunity to distance yourself from your competition," says Anders Dahlvig, Group President and CEO of IKEA Services. He had an action plan all set and approved by the board that spelled out how to take advantage of a recession. When the bottom fell out of the economy, IKEA was ready to expand their stores while competitors were forced to downsize. Ikea decided—"instead of reacting and cutting costs—to invest."

Heinz took quite the opposite tack with great success. "We concluded that the best thing to do for the company would be to shrink the company—to get smaller to get bigger, to get smaller to get better, and to get smaller to be more nimble," says William Johnson, Chairman, President and Chief Executive Officer of H.J. Heinz Company. "That's complete anathema to CEOs who immediately walk into their jobs and think the next day, 'What do I have to do to get bigger?' But before you get bigger, you have to get better." And getting better at what you do is perhaps the greatest benefit to be gained from the challenges we face today.

"Never waste a good crisis!" Deloitte Australia CEO Giam Swiegers demands. "A good crisis is when you test your team and when the opportunities occur in the market." As your competitors are frozen with indecision, this book is your call to action to take advantage of the most extraordinary opportunities for growth that you may ever see in your career.

—Mark Thompson
Bestselling coauthor of *Success Built to Last*

Crisis as Opportunity

Never Waste a Good Crisis

Giam Swiegers

CEO, Deloitte Australia

OVER THE YEARS, I've worked for many leaders—good ones and bad ones. And you can learn as much from the good ones as you can learn from the bad ones. The one time that you really see what leaders are made of is when they face difficult times.

An expression you don't get to use often if you come from where I come from is,

Crisis as Opportunity

"The one advantage of growing up in South Africa is . . ." But in difficult times, it is pretty handy to have that experience, because the advantage of getting into a leadership role in the mid-1980s in South Africa was that we were facing one crisis after another. And you learned very early in your career that you could not ignore these or celebrate these. You had to confront them and find out how you could make money out of them. If you approached these crises in an inappropriate way, you paralyzed the organization and nobody would move. My opinion has always been that you should never waste a good crisis. A good crisis is when you test your team and when the opportunities occur in the market.

One thing that's been very noticeable in facing the current credit crunch: so many of our leaders seem to think that it is their responsibility to spread the gloom or to predict an even worse outcome than the previous speaker. I have been very disappointed with some behaviors I have seen from key leaders confronting these problems. And I'm not sure how their organizations react when their people see their concern.

My view is that leaders should be realistic about the crisis they face. But make sure that everybody focuses immediately on the opportunities that arise out of that crisis and the realities of the decisions that need to be taken. And then take them really quickly. Napoleon Bonaparte said that a leader should be a dealer in hope. Ben Zander, one of the researchers whom I like, says that all leaders have the responsibility to get their people to focus on opportunity. And he says that opportunity is only one sentence away. It is just the thing that you need to say after confronting a very difficult situation.

So the key lesson for me is that you've been put into a leadership role for a reason. You are going to face difficult things. Don't get yourself and your team paralyzed. Face up to reality, decide what to do, and spot the opportunities. They're always there.

———•••———

TAKEAWAYS

———•••———

- ⚌ Difficult times are opportunities for leaders to demonstrate what they're made of.

- ⚌ Leaders should be realistic about any crisis they face, immediately focus everyone on the opportunities that arise and the realities of the decisions that need to be made, and then make decisions quickly.

- ⚌ A leader's perspective on difficult situations can mean the difference between communicating opportunity and communicating paralysis to an organization.

Be Alert to New Opportunities

J. W. Marriott Jr.

Chairman and CEO, Marriott International

THE BOY SCOUT motto is: "Be Prepared." I was a Boy Scout, and I have lots of grandchildren who are Boy Scouts and children who have been Boy Scouts. And in business, the key is: be prepared and do your homework.

We are constantly searching for opportunities. I think as you search for opportunities, and as you study what's going on in your industry and you learn what's happening, you see targets of opportunity out there that are very appealing to you. And when one comes along, you have to grab it, you have to move on it.

When we learned that Ritz-Carlton might be for sale, we moved. We learned that the owner of the company had some loans coming due, and he was a little bit short of cash. So we stepped right up and made him a loan. We worked on a contract so that we could have an opportunity to buy the company. Our competitor who was trying to buy the company as well was slow to make the loan and thought, "What's the credit? Am I going to get my money back?" And we ran in, made the loan, and made the deal.

Three months later, we closed on the Ritz-Carlton acquisition, and it's been a fantastic acquisition for us. There were thirty hotels when we bought the company. We have added thirty more, and we'll

Be Alert to New Opportunities

add another thirty in the next five years.
There will be more than one hundred
Ritz-Carlton hotels in probably another
four or five years. We are excited about that
brand, and we are using that brand not only
for hotel development but also for residen-
tial development, for condominiums, our
flag with Ritz-Carlton.

We find that there are many more brand
extensions that we have an opportunity
to work on as a result of this acquisition.
But we were ready for it. We knew what we
wanted; we knew the company, we knew
what its strengths were, we knew what its
weaknesses were; and we knew that we could
do something with this brand. What we do
in our company is constantly have a radar
going 'round—like on a ship. That radar is
always looking for opportunities. We read
a lot about what's going on in the industry,
and we target these various opportunities,
and we just keep them on our radar screen.
When one starts to ripen, we're there to get
it. And that's what we did here with Ritz.

TAKEAWAYS

⚔ As you study and learn what's going on in your industry, you will discover appealing opportunities.

⚔ Once you've identified an opportunity, move on it quickly.

⚔ Searching, preparing, and studying for opportunities can provide a critical competitive advantage in negotiating deals.

A Counterintuitive Downturn Strategy

Anders Dahlvig

Group President and CEO, IKEA Services

WHEN I STARTED AS CEO in 1999, we were in the middle of a peak in the economy. This was in the middle of the IT boom, 1999 to 2001. IKEA was doing tremendously well—I think we had a sales growth pace of 15 to 20 percent at the time. However, one of the things I learned from the mid-1990s when I was sitting further

down in the organization as a country manager when we had the downturn—a real
downturn—was that we reacted to the economy in a very short-term way; we became
very cost-focused short term. It had a
negative impact on the service we gave our
customers in the stores because we were
reducing staff and investments to try to
maximize the result in the short term.

When we were sitting there in the next
upturn in the economy in 2000, I felt it
would be good if we were planning ahead,
because after the sunshine comes the rain.
The next downturn we would see the same
effect, as always happens, but we could plan
better for it.

What we set out to do was to think about
what happens when the next downturn
comes. Could we plan different scenarios
depending on how bad it gets? The specifics
of what we did was to look at the financial
consequences if turnover went down
X percent, Y percent, or other set percent
and what our actions should be. What
we were betting on was that sales would go

down, but it wouldn't be a crisis level; it would be a downturn. And then our proposal was, instead of reacting and cutting costs, to *invest*. The proposal was that we should increase our investments in new stores compared with what we had done. We should decrease our sales prices even more, instead of pulling them up in order to save some margin. We should invest in our stores to see to it that we had the best service for our customers. We also invested in a number of measures that normally you might do in an upturn in the economy rather than a downturn.

We took this to the board and proposed that under these types of circumstances this is what we want to do—if this and this and this happen, this is what we want to do. It gave us an opportunity to have a really good discussion in a time when the economy was good, when we could confidently discuss this in the boardroom and come to some kind of agreement. And eventually we did.

Then, of course, it happened. After the IT boom, we had an IT crash. In

Crisis as Opportunity

2002–2003 the whole economy in the Western world went down pretty dramatically. And we embarked on our plan. What we did was exactly what I had proposed. We increased our expansion from around ten stores per year to twenty stores per year, which we then maintained for at least ten years, basically. We started reducing our sales prices to our customers, on average 2 to 3 percent a year—before that we had increased our prices to our customers—and we increased our store opening hours to give better service to our customers, and a number of other efforts like that.

In retrospect this has been a very successful strategy because what it did was help us to increase our distance from the competition in a way we would otherwise not have, and it put us in a totally different position. The lesson of planning for the downturn is that you are prepared when a downturn occurs and you can set your plans in motion, having the board with you and having had the discussion with your management. You don't lose time. The benefit is you don't react to the circumstances; rather you are proactively managing it in a good way. And the lesson is, if you have an offensive strategy in a downturn, like we have, it is an opportunity to distance yourself from your competition.

TAKEAWAYS

- ⚔ In times of sustained growth and a strong economy, planning your company's responses to eventual downturns is important to future successes.

- ⚔ Conducting a series of planning scenarios and developing proactive models with regard to financial consequences, before they're required, enables you to develop well thought out and successful strategies with the full support of the board.

⊰ Counterintuitively, a well-planned growth strategy can distance you from the competition during an economic downturn.

Playing a Poor Hand Well

Mary Cantando

Founder, WomanBusinessOwner.com

I BELIEVE WITH all the gifts I've been given that I have a responsibility to be upbeat regardless of the situation. I've had to put this into play many times over my career.

During the early stages of the dot-com bust, we had a Telco client who was responsible for about 25 percent of our revenue.

Crisis as Opportunity

And one day I got a call that the client was canceling our entire contract. This was really devastating news. I went into my office, sat at my desk, and quietly thought about how I was going to break the news to my staff. As I sat there, I thought, "You know, I have to find one good thing in this."

It occurred to me that they told me this client was going to pay its invoices immediately—that would help our cash flow. Also, I could move the 25 percent of the staff who were going to be freed up by this lost contract to another contract that we were ramping up—that would help us get that contract off to a good start. As much as I hated to admit it, there were some players who were a little less than A-category, and this would give me an opportunity to screen through and ensure that my whole team was top-notch.

All of a sudden, I realized that I had found three good things about a devastating situation. It also occurred to me that I could do that with anything that came across my desk, anything that came across my life.

Playing a Poor Hand Well

The very next day I had a flat tire. I got out, looked at it, and started to grouse about it. I thought, "Well, you know, Mary, you're not going to be late for a client meeting; you have a spare tire; and it's not raining. So there are three good things about having a flat tire today."

I started to embed this whole concept into my life, and I got to the point where, without even thinking about it, it happened automatically. So whenever something negative happened in my life, I would stop and say, "Well, the three good things about that are . . ." I shared this concept with all of my staff, with all my employees, and with anyone who would listen to me.

But I knew that I had hit home one day when a member of my staff, Sandra, came into my office. Her dad had just died, and it was her first day back after her bereavement leave. She came in, sat down, and said, "Mary, I want to tell you that as close as I was to my father, there are three good things about his death. This has really brought my daughter and me closer together, I learned

all about his military record that I no idea
about, and I've become incredibly close with
cousins who I didn't even know existed."

I can't tell you the sense of satisfaction
it gave me to hear Sandra's comments and
to know that I had impacted her, not only
as an employer, a boss, and a mentor but
also as a friend—I had really made a difference in her personal life as well as her
business life.

I love the story that I've heard about
Walt Disney and how, when he was creating
Disney World, he built Cinderella's Castle
first so that all the workmen who were out
in the heat dealing with the mosquitoes and
the rattlesnakes could look up and see the
goal that they were moving toward, and that
no matter how bad the situation that day,
there was some good in everything that
they were doing.

It's easy to play a good hand, but a true
master can play a poor hand well. I find that
if you can look for the good in a bad situation, it positions you to play a poor hand

well. So regardless of your business or your situation in life, when things come across your desk or your door, if you can look at them and if you can always find three good things in a situation that others will perceive as only negative, I really do believe you can be miles ahead.

TAKEAWAYS

- It's easy to play a good hand, but a true master can play a poor hand well.

- If you can look for the good in a bad situation, it positions you to exploit hidden opportunities.

- Leaders are responsible for their power to impact people beyond their working lives.

Customer Dissatisfaction Is a Great Opportunity

David Bell

Chairman Emeritus, The Interpublic Group

IT'S JUNE 2007, Heathrow Airport. The David Bell family is heading to a week of Wimbledon and has arranged for a car, through the hotel, to pick them up. The

Customer Dissatisfaction

car driver is there on time with the appropriate sign and takes us to the car, which is a minivan with ample room to accommodate several bags for four family members.

We head off toward central London, actually the West End. Everything is wonderful. We're conversing—talking about what's happening, talking about the city, past experiences—and we fall in love with our driver. As we get to Trafalgar Square and begin to approach the West End, however, it becomes very quickly obvious that there is a tentativeness on the part of the driver. He's not quite sure where the hotel is; perhaps hasn't been there before, has a general area, and is probably, although it's unspoken, going to drive around until he finds it.

This is not really a problem, except that the hotel itself is in a very difficult area, and the West End can be confusing if you don't know it. We begin driving around. After about a half hour, we realize we've gone around in circles three times. Then it becomes four times and, finally, we become

Crisis as Opportunity

a little worried, and I say, "Would you please pull over?" He doesn't pull over.

I begin to get a little more anxious and a little louder, and I start to beg him. He doesn't pull over. He begins to hyperventilate. He begins to get anxious and visibly tense, which speeds up his driving, and yet he's still won't stop. After forty-five minutes of driving around in, essentially, the same area, without any direction and his refusal to stop, we begin to scream. The family rolls down the window and yells for the police. I finally get him to pull over, as my son is pushing the bags out the door into the Covent Garden area to escape what appears to be a semirabid lunatic. Everyone is scared to death.

We walk, with bags, the rest of the way to the hotel. We have no trouble getting directions. But the family is frightened that, because we have been so angry with the driver, perhaps he'll look for some retribution.

Actually, what happened in this lesson is one of the greatest disruption cases for customer satisfaction I've ever seen.

Customer Dissatisfaction

When I arise the next morning,
outside the door is an envelope that says,
"Mr. Bell." I open it up, and it is a heartfelt
apology from the driver, who says that it's all
his fault, that he shouldn't have done it, and
would I please accept his apology. Interest-
ing way to start the morning.

After returning to the room from outside
the front door, there's a call from the owner
of the company, who has heard about the
problem and who says that the ride is free
and that the ride back to Heathrow is free.
He apologizes and says that he had given
explicit directions to the driver, who was
new, who obviously hadn't paid attention.
All this sounds wonderful, except I negoti-
ate that the driver who'd taken us in not take
us to the airport. I say that we'll be happy
to pay at least half of it because he did get
us most of the way.

But, importantly, the lesson on disruption was, on our appointed pickup to go
back to Heathrow a week later, the owner of
the company is out front with an envelope
filled with cash to give me and to personally

apologize to me for the inconvenience. As you can imagine, I took his card and, in the future, whenever I need a driver in the London area, his will be the company I will call.

The lesson is clear. Anytime there is a lack of customer satisfaction, there is an enormous opportunity to create loyalty by exactly what you do with the disruption.

TAKEAWAYS

⚜ Customer dissatisfaction is a prime opportunity for improving customer service.

⚜ Appropriate acknowledgment and response to customer dissatisfaction can actually create customer retention and loyalty.

Embracing Conflict

Richard Pascale

*Associate Fellow, Saïd Business School,
Oxford University*

IT'S THE LATE 1960s; Lyndon Johnson
is president. I'm in the middle of my graduate work at Harvard Business School, and
I have a chance to go to Washington as a
White House Fellow for a year, which is
where you get to be the special assistant
to a cabinet member. In this case I was

working for the Secretary of Labor during the great days of the Great Society when the Department of Labor was really an engine of action.

I arrive on the scene and find myself spending a lot of time with the senior civil servants in the department, most of whom were guys who had spent their lives either dealing with collective bargaining negotiations or with mediation. Now, here I was, midway in an academic career, studying strategic transformation and organizational behavior and, I thought, reasonably up to speed on the major ideas on change and organizational effectiveness.

Suddenly, two months into this experience, I find myself surrounded by people who had a whole different paradigm. It dawned on me gradually that these folks saw conflict as a source of renewal and a valuable asset to an organization, a kind of fuel. And their skill in dealing with conflict and teasing it out, making use of it rather than gliding over it, was something to behold. It was a hugely important wake-up call for me.

Embracing Conflict

Indeed, it became the subject of a course on conflict and negotiation that I taught at Stanford for fifteen years.

I came to see conflict as an incredibly important force for creating a necessary kind of disequilibrium that allows people and organizations to learn. This leads to the three key points, which are: first, a premise of mine, that prolonged equilibrium is a precursor to death. I mean, certainly in the natural world—and, indeed, in organizations—when you're in a niche for a long time that is fairly stable, there's a strong tendency for a species or for an organization to become overly adaptive. You become so comfortable and so well suited for a particular niche that, when the world changes around you, you're actually maladaptive to the new environment.

One of the corollary rules here is that you have to be smarter than your food. Often, as an organization, your food changes, or other people compete for it; and being smarter than that food requires something to get you out of your comfort zone. Conflict is a fabulous fuel for doing that.

The second point is to really listen to the hidden conflict, because most organizations shy away from it, submerge it, smooth it over, and avoid it. Or, in some cases, "fight and reload" becomes the dominant means, where they go to battle with great vigor only to rearm and go back to working with no real resolution. But the ability to confront and problem-solve is at the heart of the task if, per point two, you're trying to make conflict work for you.

The third point is that you need to look for the hidden tensions that organizations essentially have to embrace, between people who want things centralized so they can control them and the people who need lots of latitude and decentralization; between an approach to the future that's opportunistic versus people who really want a nailed-down game plan and to know where their strategy is taking them. We swim in these tensions within organizations. If you seize on these as a means of moving an organization forward and use the tension as a wake-up call, it can be very powerful.

TAKEAWAYS

⚐ Conflict is an essential force for creating the disequilibrium that allows people and organizations to learn and grow.

⚐ Prolonged equilibrium can harm an organization in the long run by making it maladaptive to changing environments.

⚐ All organizations contain hidden tensions that, if identified and embraced, can be powerful catalysts for forward momentum.

Change Is Good

David Brandon

Chairman and CEO, Domino's Pizza

EARLY IN MY LIFE I was a student athlete at the University of Michigan, and it was a wonderful opportunity for me to get my first lessons in the world of management because I had great coaches. I played on a football team that won thirty games, lost one, and tied one in three years. We won the championship all three years, so it was a very high level of performance, great

Change Is Good

coaches, and a lot of really good players.
I didn't play a lot in those days. I was on
the team and I was proud to be so, but
I got a chance to observe a lot—sometimes
more than I wanted to—from the perspective
of how the coaches prepared the team
to win.

One of the things that fascinated me was
that, in the game of football, there is a situation that's probably one of the hardest
to deal with and is what we call "sudden
change." What it meant was that the defense
would come off the field and they'd be
tired; they'd be looking for water, and
they'd want to sit down and rest. They
wouldn't even get to the spot on the bench
where they'd be comfortable before the
offense would fumble the ball or throw an
interception, or have some situation occur
that would be the most negative thing for
a defense you could imagine, because it
meant they had to go right back out there
without any rest and usually defend in a
situation that was very, very negative.

Crisis as Opportunity

What I found fascinating was that the coaches were actually able to forecast that this was going to happen throughout the season, and they prepared the team for it. At practice we used to go through mock drills of sudden change. What they taught us to do whenever that nasty situation occurred was to all shout "Sudden change!" And we would all get together as a team, grab hands, and seize this as an opportunity. In other words, we were programmed to believe that when this very negative situation occurred, rather than responding negatively we would actually see it as an opportunity, get excited about it, and anticipate it in a way that we knew we were going to be successful.

I later in life determined that that was a great lesson that could be applied to the world of business. Because if organizations understand that change is good, and when you are confronted with change— particularly change that is challenging— a great organization is going to be ready for that; they're going to anticipate it and see it as an opportunity. I really adopted my own version of sudden change in business, and my phrase is called "Change is good."

Throughout my organization, whenever we encounter something that was not anticipated, particularly something that has some negative connotations to it, we'll look at one another and say, "Change is good. This is an opportunity for us to react to change, make it positive, and apply ourselves in a way that allows us to step up and accomplish something important."

We tend to resist change because often change creates problems that require solutions, and sometimes those solutions require a lot of extra work. So if you understand that people are going to approach change with trepidation and some are going to resist it, I think as a leader the way that you can best prepare your organization is to transform their thinking and put them in a mindset that makes them want to embrace change.

TAKEAWAYS

- ⚵ Forecasting and preparing for sudden change is an important leadership skill.

- ⚵ Disruptive change can be an important opportunity for an organization to create successful outcomes.

- ⚵ One of the best ways to prepare an organization for change, particularly where the change is perceived as negative, is to promote a mind-set that wants to embrace it.

Leadership Is Not a Popularity Contest

Sanjiv Ahuja

Chairman, Orange UK

THERE IS A BIG myth in business that you need buy-in of your strategy from your team; and also I think there's a big myth believed by leaders that they need to win the popularity contest inside a company. As a leader of a business, be very clear in your mind that you are not running a democracy. By virtue of the fact that you have been anointed the leader, there is a significant degree of autocracy that comes with you. When you make decisions and when you make choices, they're not always the most popular.

If your objective is to ensure that your team buys into your strategy and likes what you do, then candidly you are not needed as a leader. You could do a continuous poll and determine what decisions and direction the company ought to take—do it from morning until night and then everybody votes on it—and the business goes wherever.

You, as a leader, are supposed to make some decisions that are necessarily not going to be very popular, and that's okay; but stand up and be counted for those decisions. Sometimes those decisions are where you bet your job, but that's okay; stand up and be counted for those. Look in the history of mankind; all successful leaders at different stages of their lives have made those decisions. In our efforts, these are

Leadership Is Not a Popularity Contest

"bet-your-job" decisions, and that's okay; people sometimes have to make "bet-your-life" decisions.

Some of us make decisions successfully, some unsuccessfully, but most of the decisions we make are not that critical. But you must make decisions and not get deluded with the absolute myth that you need to be a popular leader. You need to be an effective leader; you need to be a decisive leader. And while you are leading with effectiveness, decisiveness, clarity, and the passion for the success of your business, your team eventually does follow you. I'll give you an example.

Ten years ago I was brought into a business where employee morale was down, product quality was down, the profits were in a terrible shape, and the revenue had been in decline for many years. Most of the customers thought that it wasn't a business that could be turned around; most of the employees thought it wasn't a business that could be turned around either. When I stepped in, I had to make a significant number of changes. I changed most of the leadership team, I changed a good part of the management team that worked for those leaders, and essentially I restructured the business.

In the early days, I probably wasn't the most popular leader. Actually, I *know* I was not the most popular leader. But by the time we finished the transformation, the company was delivering world-class performance in the area it was engaged in, in terms of quality, delivery, productivity, profitability, and growth. In all criteria, it was performing in a world-class manner, and I would like to say that by the time I left I was probably the most popular leader that company had ever had. But if I were looking for employee polls, I probably wouldn't have made any of the tough decisions that I had to make.

For all leaders in all situations, you have to make the tough calls; but stand up for those and be counted. Don't shy away, and don't get confused between popularity and

the right choices. Right choices and popularity do not have to go hand in hand.

TAKEAWAYS

- ⚐ Leaders should stand up and be
  counted for the difficult decisions
  that they make.

- ⚐ Do not confuse a popular decision
  with a right decision; many times
  the right decision for a leader to make
  will be an unpopular one.

- ⚐ Teams will eventually follow those who
  lead with effectiveness, decisiveness,
  clarity, and a passion for the success
  of their business.

Having the Courage of Your Convictions

Amelia Fawcett

Chairman, Pensions First

ANYBODY CAN MAKE an easy decision. I think what probably defines true managers are those who are able to make quite difficult choices.

I remember at the end of 1993, we'd had a record year at the firm. Our then chairman, Dick Fisher, decided that we needed to make a significant investment—particularly in headcount—to make a quantum leap in market share for the firm. This was very much in sync with his oft-articulated strategy and view that the firm was globalizing fast, as were our clients, and in order to be successful we needed to be as strong in local markets as we were globally. And we were a little behind in some markets.

So the decree went out that people should look and come back with suggestions on where they wanted to add headcount, and where they were light on the ground and needed to invest to make a meaningful difference in that relevant market. The plans were approved, and everybody started hiring people. It was a particularly important time for Europe, where we were a bit underinvested, and a lot of the resources came our way.

However, in 1994, there was the Mexican debt crisis, and the financial markets had a major wobble. Many financial services firms were staring at potentially significantly reduced revenues and income, and they started to pull back. We looked to Dick and said, "Well, in this kind of environment should we continue?" And he said, "Yes; our long-term strategy is right—continue." So we continued to hire, and then the markets got worse and most of our competitors started laying people off. Again people said, "Do you really want us to continue?" And he replied, "Absolutely; the strategic imperative is the same."

By the end of 1994, which was indeed a tough year, despite howls of protest from industry analysts—and a fair amount of skepticism within certain quarters of the firm—we had completed our plan and added 15 percent to our headcount. That was a significant amount at the time. And in 1995 and 1996, we took very large amounts of market share in almost every major market—particularly the markets outside the United States.

Frankly, the foundation for the growth that we've had since then—particularly here

Having the Courage of Your Convictions

in Europe—was clearly set in the investments that we made at that time. I think Dick, and the courage of his convictions, were an inspiration to me and to many others at Morgan Stanley. It was a powerful example of why, in addition to short-term opportunities and focus on growth and profitability, you need to remember where you're going and what your long-term investment and strategic goals are. At the end of the day, despite difficulties in the market, if you still believe that the fundamental, strategic direction is correct, you have to have the courage of your convictions and stay the course, regardless of how unpopular people might think that decision is.

In 1994 we made a bet on Russia that if you were going to service and be important in the natural gas industry, you had to be able to understand it and be a player there. So we built an office and, in the mid-1990s, started to add more people. But in 1998, with the Russian debt crisis, it became clear that that was going to be a serious problem and potentially a cost that many firms weren't willing to take. But we still felt that, over the longer term, you could not be a player in the natural resources industry without understanding and being a part of the Russian scene.

So unlike our competitors, we stayed the course. We trimmed the office down some-what. We put our growth plans on hold, but we kept the office and its people there, and we maintained a focus on our clients there when most of our competitors closed their office and fired their staff. That meant that we were able to maintain, and still have, a leading franchise; it's only recently that our competitors have returned.

Anyone can make decisions. We all make decisions every day, but so do the people who work for us. The real test is people who can make difficult decisions, who can stand up to unpopular decisions and criticism, and who have the courage of their convic-tions to do what they think is right and keep in mind the strategic long-term goal.

TAKEAWAYS

⚔ The ability to make decisions is
   truly tested when those decisions
   are difficult, unpopular, and subject
   to criticism.

⚔ Long-term strategic goals can guide
   and fortify your conviction in the
   rightness of your decisions.

⚔ Once a decision is made, it is important to stay the course without regard
   to what others are doing if you still
   believe your course is the right one.

The Counterintuitive Strategy

William Johnson

Chairman, President, and CEO,
H.J. Heinz Company

A STRATEGY IS THE cornerstone of any business. Execution is what wins games, but strategy determines the playbook. In the case of Heinz, all strategy begins with an understanding of the markets we're in and the environment.

The best example for us was a major transaction in 2002 when we spun off a big piece of our company to Del Monte in what at the time was called a reverse Morris trust, which was a unique way to satisfy multiple constituents. We needed to change our portfolio. Our portfolio was not right. We were in businesses where we were disadvantaged and couldn't win. We needed to be in businesses where we were well positioned and could win.

As we went through a quick survey of the company and did some detailed analysis work as a follow-up, we concluded that there were three businesses where we were advantaged and could bring certain leverage to bear and thereby create value. There were a few businesses where we were not advantaged—those being pet food, tuna, and a private-label soup business in the United States where we were competing against people who were just better than we were.

Crisis as Opportunity

We concluded that the best thing to do for the company would be to shrink the company—to get smaller to get bigger, to get smaller to get better, and to get smaller to be more nimble. Interestingly enough, that's complete anathema to CEOs who immediately walk into their jobs and think the next day, "What do I have to do to get bigger?" Before you get bigger, you have to get better.

This shrinking was a step we took to get better. It was based on an understanding of the industry, an understanding of our customers. We talked to a number of customers and consumers, and we did a complete peer analysis to understand where we were advantaged. We did a geographic review to understand where we could grow, wouldn't grow, and how all these business parts fit in.

Fundamentally, what determines your strategy is courage. You have to have the courage of convictions and the courage to move. You can analyze all you want, and you can research all you want. If research was always right, nobody would ever make a mistake; therefore by definition it can't always be right. We did a lot of analysis and a lot of work, but fundamentally it comes down to judgment based on the information—less-than-perfect information—and the ability to move on. That's probably the most important transaction this company has ever undertaken, and it changed this business immensely.

One of the learnings we had was not so positive. We did not do a good job of communicating to our multiple constituents what we were trying to do—primarily, in this case, Wall Street. We took a leap of faith and took for granted that Wall Street would understand that this was a multiyear process. They didn't. The market is driven on a quarter-to-quarter basis; and we, being driven on a long-term strategic basis, did not do the job adequately of communicating to the industry the benefits of what we were going to do and how long it was going to take. As a consequence, impatience set

in about halfway through the process.
We're obviously over that now, the
results have been seen, and the business
is responding brilliantly. But overcommu-
nicating is part of that process and strategy.

The second thing we learned to do after
the fact is engage multiple constituents.
You not only have to engage your employees, but you also have to engage your
customers, your consumers, the Street,
and other people just to make sure that
everyone is marching in lock step in the
same direction. The single biggest differen-
tiation between a successful strategy and
one that fails is that in the failed one there
is an inability to get everybody talking,
working, and marching together. That
is a key learning.

The other thing I've learned in all strategy settings, and the thing that amazes me
more than anything, is how poorly read
members of the senior management team
are. You have to read. I'm always kidding
the people who work for me—and I have

The Counterintuitive Strategy

numerous instances of this—that they can
read *BusinessWeek* and *Fortune* all they want,
but it won't do them any good because those
are after-the-fact reports. They need to be
reading *People* and *National Enquirer* and their
local newspaper because those publications
foretell what's going to happen.

Part and parcel of a good strategy and
effective management is an understanding
of what you're good at and what you're not.
You need an objective, honest appraisal of
how you get to what you're good at and dis-
pense with things you're not good at. While
it was anathema to us to shrink the company, the reality was that parts of the company were sick, not performing well,
brought no strategic skill whatsoever, and
certainly had no executional benefits. They
were clearly going to encumber the parts
of the business that were operative and
strategically advantaged. As a result we'd
never get to the advantaged part because
we'd be spending so much time worrying
about the disadvantaged part.

TAKEAWAYS

✂ An understanding of your strengths and weaknesses based on facts and sound analysis underlies good strategy and effective management.

✂ Counterintuitively, it may be necessary for a company to become smaller, even temporarily, in order to achieve its strategic objectives over the long term.

✂ In embarking upon a new or counterintuitive strategy, you should overcommunicate your plan to shareholders, stakeholders, and constituents who may not understand its benefits.

Creating a Common Language for a New Course of Action

Clayton Christensen

Robert and Jane Cizik Professor of Business Administration, Harvard Business School

THE RESEARCH I'VE done shows that what cripples successful, well-run companies isn't that some competitor comes into their market with a better

product. Rather, what cripples them
is when somebody comes into the bottom
of the market, making a product that is
much cheaper and simpler, which then
takes root in undemanding applications
and moves up. A midlevel engineer at Intel,
who read an early academic paper I wrote,
said she looked down at the bottom of her
market, and there was one of these competitors coming at Intel. It was Syrex, which
had begun selling much cheaper micro-
processors into the least-profitable tier
of the market for entry-level computer
systems.

Intel was just getting out of that business
because if they got out of the entry-level
products, they were lopping off the low-
profit end of their product line and,
therefore, improving their reported
profit margins. But you could see Syrex
continuing to come up market because
that was the path for them: improving
their gross margins. It actually was a perfect
replica of the stuff that I had seen in my
other research.

Creating a Common Language

This engineer, Carmen Nagito, coordi-
nated a meeting for me with Andy Grove
and the executive staff of Intel. In about a
two-hour meeting, I think they came to see
that—oh my gosh!—this would do to Intel
what Toyota did to General Motors, what
Cisco did to Lucent. And it's a serious
thing. As he applied my research models
to his own environment, Andy reached the
decision that Intel needed to come down
to the bottom of the market and launch a
product that they now call the Celeron chip.
And Intel needed to get into a new business
called *flash memory*, a very new business in the
mid-1990s. Both of these things were very
counter to the logic of Intel, because they
entailed going to lower-margin business
rather than higher-margin business. The
financial structure and the reward structure
were oriented toward improving gross profit
margins.

Well, I was interested that even though
Andy had such power in the company—
both positional power and intellectual
horsepower—once he understood what

Crisis as Opportunity

Intel had to do, he didn't just stand up on his chair and say, "Guys, this is where we're going." Rather, working through their corporate training program, they set up a series of seminars that lasted for a whole day—eighteen of these seminars over the course of a year—and they brought in about a hundred managers to each seminar. In the beginning, I led those seminars myself but then gradually turned them over to Andy and other members of the staff.

I'd present a little bit about my model of disruption, and then we'd have breakout groups for the people to consider, "Is Intel really getting disrupted, and what does it mean for our future?" I'd present a little bit more, and we'd go into the breakout groups for them to explore how Intel could disrupt other people and create new growth businesses. This is where the insight came that flash memory was going to disrupt disk drives. Then I'd present a little bit more, and we had breakout groups again to explore the question, "How does Intel need to change the way it's organized so that it can create new growth businesses by disrupting others and defend itself against the disruption from Syrex?" Over the course of the year, we took about two thousand of Intel's midlevel and senior managers through this training program.

Last year, Intel booked about $16 billion in new business from ideas that bubbled up out of those breakout group discussions. Intel would be a very troubled company today had they not had those growth agents.

I had a chance to talk to Andy a couple of years ago about how he had pulled all of this off, and he said, "You know, your models—they didn't give us any answers to our questions, but they gave us a common language and a common way to frame the problem, so we could reach consensus around a counterintuitive course of action." I just thought that was brilliant because if, in fact, the people in the organization don't have a common language and a common way to frame their problem, then they're all proposing solutions to different kinds of problems because they don't have an insight about what's causing this situation.

If you really want to implement a new course of action effectively, actually giving the whole management team the language and the understanding of the root cause of what's happening just allows consensus to coalesce. I decided then that there really was a role for people like me in the world, whose work was to give other people a methodology to correctly frame the problems, in a language around which they could coalesce on a course of action.

TAKEAWAYS

⚔ What disrupts successful, well-run companies is not the introduction of new and better products from competitors; it is the introduction of cheaper, simpler products into the bottom of a market, which then take root in undemanding applications and move up.

⌘ To implement a new course of action effectively, give your whole management team a common language and a common understanding of the root issue you intend to address, which allows consensus to simply coalesce.

⌘ A company can generate significant profit from exploring ideas for new business from within.

Finding Solutions for a Successful Turnaround

Paul Anderson

Chairman, Spectra Energy

MY GREATEST BUSINESS challenge was probably when I took over BHP Billiton in 1998. At the time, BHP was a conglomerate; it was primarily involved in mining, but it also had large steel and petroleum businesses.

The company was in total disarray. The stock price had lost half of its market value, and the CEO who preceded me had been fired, so the company had been leaderless for about nine months. It was reviled by the press and by all stock analysts, who were very upset with the company's course. BHP was involved in a number of projects that had no hope of profitability, were losing money, behind schedule, and over budget. It was even the poster child for environmentalists: it had a huge environmental problem in Papua New Guinea where the western province was suffering from a large copper project that they had there. When you looked at it, you knew this was a company in trouble.

By the time I arrived in Australia, I was asking myself what I was doing there. I was taking on a new company, a new country, and a new industry. I didn't have much mining experience at that point in time, and I knew absolutely no one in the company. I had interviewed with the board, but I did not know a single company manager. So it was a pretty exciting adventure to emigrate to another country and take on a task like this.

Since I knew nothing, I figured I'd better do some information gathering. I gathered together the top eighty managers in the company. They had an Executive Leadership Group, so I figured it would be a good place to start. I said to the group, "I don't know too much about what's going on here, but I assume that you do. I'd like each of you to give me two pieces of paper.

"On one piece, tell me a bit about yourself, your background, what you're responsible for, the challenges that you're facing, what your group is expected to do over the next year or two; mainly, what might surprise me with regard to your activity. But on the second piece of paper, tell me what you would do if you were CEO of this company. If you had absolutely no restrictions and total authority, what would you do with this company?"

Finding Solutions

I sat down with those eighty people, spending anywhere from an hour to a day with each one of them. I reviewed those two pages, absorbed as much information as I could, and then synthesized a strategy for the company out of all that input. To cut a long story short, two-and-a-half years later the company was thriving: we had record profits; the stock price had more than doubled. We had merged with Billiton and created, at that point, the largest resources company in the world, dual-listed in London and Australia. It was very much a success story. People asked me, "How did you get from point A to point B? What created that success?"

As I look back on it, I realize there was nothing we did that wasn't on those two pages. The organization knew exactly what needed to be done; there were no silver bullets, no new, clever ideas. The organization really understood what needed to be done; they just couldn't implement it for a number of reasons. They didn't understand the mosaic or how it all fitted together; they had pieces of it but not the whole picture. They might not think they had the authority. It might not be in their area of responsibility. In many cases, they just lacked the permission or the courage to do it. It was merely having someone come in and say, "You can do this; yes, it is going to cause a large write-off if we move out of Papua New Guinea, and that will be a shock to the shareholders, but the alternative is much worse."

Giving them that permission and the value judgments allowed them to go ahead and take those actions. The lesson to me was that when you come into a situation, don't think you have the answers, because one person can't possibly have all the answers relative to the knowledge that exists within that organization. But the answers do exist within that organization. Your job is to seek them out, put them together, and synthesize a strategy from them.

------◆◆◆------

TAKEAWAYS

------◆◆◆------

❧ When you approach a new situation, don't think you have all the answers.

❧ One person's knowledge cannot compete with the knowledge that exists within an entire organization.

❧ As a leader, your job is to extract organizational knowledge and synthesize what's of value into a strategy that you enable others to implement and execute.

Being Honest Prevents Failure and Amplifies Opportunity

Robin Chase

Founder and Former CEO, Zipcar

I THINK IT'S CRITICAL that companies think of themselves as learning companies. And as part of that concept, each one of us has to have, what I consider to be, intellectual honesty. We need to be able to look at any decision we've made or any of our weaknesses, and address them. So, as CEO, you have to be able to think, "I'm rotten at this, so I'm going to hire someone to fill those gaps."

As we build our companies, for the most part, we don't really know how to do what we're doing. If you're doing something for the first time or it's a new industry, as it was for us, you have all sorts of ideas, but you're trying to do it better than your competition, so that your offering is novel.

My feeling is that you can do all sorts of experiments. Experiments are fine, and no one should be getting in trouble for doing experiments. But they should get in trouble if they don't go back and look to see how that experiment came out. I think market-ing is a prime example of that. You spend these marketing dollars on whatever it is; but then you look and say, "Did that play out? Was it worthwhile?" If it's going really well and you feel as if you've found some-thing, then do a lot more of it. If it's

crummy, end it, learn your lesson, and
keep going.

One of my favorite stories—as in the
worst day of my Zipcar career—occurred
very early on. I was three weeks away from
closing my series A round for $1.3 million.
So all that money was there and promised,
and we were just finishing up the paper-
work. And at that time, I had had my first
significant month of people using the service, so I could look at my business model
and say, "Okay, we've had this much use
of the vehicles. Let's see how much revenue
we got of off that much use." I could test my
assumptions.

The absolutely horrible thing was that
I got way less revenue out of the utilization
I saw, so it was way worse than I thought.
And it was this horrible moment when I
thought, "I'm selling this complete bill of
goods. How can I take this money? There
is no business model here. I've completely
screwed it up." And I wept. Then I went
into a room by myself and chilled for

Being Honest Prevents Failure

a while. And then I dragged myself out,
and we looked at the spreadsheets.

We looked at all the numbers and realized
that when we had been calculating utilization in our forecasts, a twenty-four-hour
daily rate was not like twenty-four-hour
hourly rates. It's, in fact, much less because
you have a cap. Our daily rate was just too
low. We had at that time, I think, 450 members, which was not very many, but it was
450 people who were using our services.
They had just signed on, and we were going
to tell them, "What you signed on for,
sorry, we're not giving you that price. We're
raising it by a lot of money." We were going
to raise the daily rates, I think, by something
like 20 percent. And it was causing the staff
and us a huge amount of angst.

But when I looked at it, I thought, we can
either pretend it isn't a problem, and we can
go another year and the company will go
into bankruptcy, or we can face reality: we
screwed up—wrong price point—and we have
to change it. So we did. We sent an e-mail to

all the members, and I said that I was
really sorry, but I had to raise the daily rates
20 percent; and that it was kind of embar-
rassing to tell them this, but the business
wasn't viable without that kind of rate;
and that this was what I had to do.

I came into work the next day with a
pounding heart. I thought, "How many
people are going to send me flaming
e-mails and say, 'You know, you completely
lied to us, and we're leaving the service'"?
Instead, I got a huge flood of e-mails from
people who said, "Don't worry, Robin,
we're behind you all the way. We think it's a
great service, and we're still going to use it;
that price is no problem." It was really an
amazing experience, really a heartwarming
experience.

But from an experiential and learning
point of view, when you get these nasty
surprises—and you will—don't be an ostrich
and stick your head in the sand. You really
have to correct them; you really have to
deal with them; and the sooner you do it,
the better.

Being Honest Prevents Failure

Being a learning organization is actually
one of the keys to success and probably
the most important thing of anything
that I have to say. It allows you to take risks
because you're going to catch the failures
and amplify the opportunities. I think it
has repercussions for staffing, for finance,
and for understanding your business model
through and through, which you need
to do, so I can't emphasize it enough.

TAKEAWAYS

⊰ In order to identify and correct
  failures, as well as to amplify opportunities, it is critical that a company
  perceive itself as a learning company.

⊰ A learning company must examine its
  decisions and its weaknesses with intellectual honesty.

Crisis as Opportunity

⚑ Do not avoid or ignore mistakes or failures, but correct them as quickly as possible, regardless of short-term discomfort and fear.

Involving Customers in the Change Process

Ken Freeman

Former Chairman and CEO, Quest Diagnostics

ONE OF THE FIRST turnarounds I ran, which was in the business of making CRTs— the large, heavy glass components that go into traditional television sets—was a huge wake-up call for me. When I arrived in the business around 1990, it was about

Crisis as Opportunity

$350 million in size. We were one of only
a couple of glassmakers left in the United
States. I had only seven customers. I could
call my seven large customers in twenty
minutes. I could introduce myself, and
did, to my large customers upon arrival
in the business.

I'll never forget one of those calls,
which was with Philips, the company
headquartered in The Netherlands; our
biggest customer. They bought more than
60 percent of the glass coming out of our
largest factory, located in State College,
Pennsylvania.

On the phone, I was introducing
myself and said, "I'm the new guy. I'm the
new CEO of this joint venture Corning
has with a Japanese company"—the joint
venture being called Corning Asahi Video
Products. "You don't know me, but I want
to thank you for your business. I understand our contract to work together on
an exclusive basis is expiring in about six
or seven months, and I look forward to
meeting you."

Involving Customers

All of a sudden, Dr. Eva Wilson, the president of the CRT tube-making division of Philips, interrupted me and said, "Ken, you're about the fourth CEO I've talked to in the last six years. I'm not holding that against you, but the door's been revolving pretty rapidly over there. Corning's joint ventured the business, so it only owns 51 percent today, and when I took over running Philips' CRT division for tubes, Corning owned the whole business. Worse yet, Ken, the quality of the glass you're sending me, which I use to manufacture picture tubes, is the worst in the world. No one makes it worse than Corning. So what I want you to know, Ken, and don't take it personally, is that while you're busy at Corning Asahi Video Products trying to get by with poor quality, I'm busy trying to get by without you."

I went to our factory in State College and began spreading the message about how our biggest customer was telling me that our quality was awful and that they were doing everything they could to walk away from us

in only six months. The reaction from
employees as I met with them in town
meetings—and this was a factory of about
twenty-five hundred employees—was consis-
tent. They said, "Ken, Corning invented
color television glass back in the 1950s with
RCA. We've seen threats before. We've been
in business now for thirty years. You're the
fifth CEO we've seen in about ten years.
We'll outlast you. We hear you, but we're
not listening."

Well, I had to do something very dramatic
if I was going to get the employees of our
company to listen to the intensity of the
need from our customers. I had to do
something very different. So I decided to
shut down the factory for nine days. And
rather than trying as hard as I might to get
our employee base to listen to the intensity
of the message and the concern from the
message itself and the need for change,
I asked for, and got, our biggest customers
to come to Pennsylvania to meet with our
employees in three different three-day ses-
sions, to share with our employee base the

fact that we needed to change or we would disappear.

The customers came; we shut the factory down. My supervisors and superiors in Corning thought I was crazy, because it was costing us millions and millions of dollars a day in lost production. When our employees initially heard this, their chairs weren't even facing the stage; they didn't want to hear from management. But when the customers began to talk, you could see our employees begin to change. They began turning their chairs; they began listening to our customers and interacting.

On the first day, we unfroze our employees; the second day, we began articulating a vision for the future together; and by the third day, our employees were coming up with the solutions to improve our quality, responsiveness, and service so that we could stay in the game—which, in fact, is what we did as we renewed our contract with Philips, built our business over the next three years, and restored profitability to a business that had not been profitable for fifteen consecutive years. It started by getting our employees focused on the customer.

The lesson from this story is reasonably self-evident, and that is: employee satisfaction yields customer satisfaction; and customer satisfaction, in the end, yields shareholder satisfaction. Sounds simple, but it is so often ignored. As we think about the notion of employee satisfaction, customer satisfaction, and shareholder satisfaction, everything starts with having an employee base that's ready to change, that wants to change, and that knows why they come to work every single day.

TAKEAWAYS

⊰ In times of poor product performance, getting employees focused on the customer is key to a return to profitability.

Involving Customers

⚏ Leaders must act inventively to reach their employees and articulate a vision that encourages their active participation in customer-focused change.

⚏ Employee satisfaction produces customer satisfaction, which ultimately yields increased profitability and improved shareholder satisfaction.

⊰ ABOUT THE ⊱ CONTRIBUTORS

Sanjiv Ahuja is the Chairman of Orange UK,
a position he has held since stepping down as
CEO of Orange SA.

He is the Founder and Chairman of Augere,
a new venture aiming to provide broadband access
for all. He is also a Director for ITU Telecom.

Mr. Ahuja served as CEO of Orange SA from
March 2004 to April 2007. Prior to that, he was
the company's Chief Operating Officer from
April 2003 to March 2004. During his leadership,
Orange increased the number of countries in which
it operates from seventeen to twenty-three, and
more than doubled the number of its mobile customers—from 48 million to more than 100 million
worldwide. Mr. Ahuja has also overseen the successful extension of the Orange brand from its mobile
origins so that it now embraces France Telecom's
broadband, fixed line, and IPTV services in its
largest markets.

Mr. Ahuja's previous industry experience
includes the role of President of Telcordia Technologies (formerly Bellcore), the world's largest
provider of operations support systems, network
software, and consulting and engineering services

to the telecommunications industry. Before that, he spent fifteen years at IBM in various executive roles. His last responsibility included leading IBM's entry into the telecommunications software industry.

Mr. Ahuja has a degree in electrical engineering from Delhi University, India, and a master's degree from Columbia University in New York.

Paul Anderson is the Chairman of Spectra Energy. Mr. Anderson is also a Director of Qantas Airways and BHP Billiton, a global resources company.

Mr. Anderson started his career at Ford Motor Company, holding various positions from 1969 to 1972. He was Planning Manager from 1972 until 1977, and then joined PanEnergy. Over the ensuing years, Mr. Anderson served in various leadership roles within PanEnergy, culminating in becoming its Chairman, President, and CEO.

In 1998 Mr. Anderson moved to BHP, where he was Managing Director and CEO until its merger with Billiton in 2001. He then became Managing Director and CEO of BHP Billiton until his retirement from the company in 2002.

Mr. Anderson returned to Duke Energy as Chairman and CEO in November 2003. He became Chairman of Spectra Energy in 2007 when Duke Energy's natural gas business was spun off into a new company called Spectra Energy.

David Bell is Chairman Emeritus and previously served as Vice Chairman and CEO of The Interpublic Group, one of the world's largest marketing communications and services companies. He is also currently an Operating Advisor at Pegasus Capital Advisors, L.P., a private equity fund manager.

Mr. Bell previously held the positions of Chairman and CEO of True North Communications, Inc., the world's sixth-largest global advertising and marketing communications holding company; President and CEO of Bozell Worldwide, where he helped grow the agency from $12 million to over $500 million in revenues; and President of Knox Reeves Advertising.

Mr. Bell serves as a Director for Primedia, Inc., Director for Lighting Science Group Corporation, and Director for Warnaco Group, Inc. He was inducted into the Advertising Hall of Fame in March 2007 and is the author of *Achieving Success as an Advertising Team*.

David Brandon is the Chairman and CEO of Domino's Pizza, a recognized world leader in pizza delivery operating a network of company-owned and franchise-owned stores throughout the world.

Mr. Brandon started his career at Procter & Gamble, where he worked in sales management. In 1979, following his tenure at P&G, he moved to Valassis Communications, Inc., a company in the sales-promotion and coupon industries. He became President and CEO in 1989, a position he held until 1998, while additionally taking on the role of Chairman in the last two years.

About the Contributors

Mr. Brandon subsequently moved to Domino's Pizza, and has been the company's Chairman and CEO since March 1999.

Mary Cantando is the Founder of WomanBusiness-Owner.com, a national advisory firm that focuses on helping women-owned businesses expand.

Ms. Cantando has more than twelve years' experience as an entrepreneurial executive, and spent six years researching women business owners. She is a nationally recognized expert on growing women-owned businesses.

In addition she holds a seat on the National Board of the Women Presidents' Organization, an association of women who own multimillion-dollar businesses. She is also a member of the National Women's Forum, is certified by the Women's Business Enterprise National Council, and is a member of Women Impacting Public Policy.

Ms. Cantando is the author of *The Woman's Advantage: 20 Women Entrepreneurs Show You What It Takes to Grow Your Business* and *Nine Lives: Stories of Women Business Owners Landing on Their Feet*.

Robin Chase is Founder and CEO of Meadow Networks, as well as Founder and CEO of GoLoco.org. She is also Founder and former CEO of Zipcar, a company that offers car rentals by the hour.

In June 2000, Ms. Chase cofounded Zipcar. She stepped down as CEO in 2003, at which point she founded and became CEO of Meadow

About the Contributors

Networks, a consultancy that applies wireless technologies to transportation. She later founded GoLoco, a ride-sharing service, to fill the consumer need to share car travel and costs, and to reduce emissions.

Ms. Chase is a frequent lecturer and has been featured on the *Today Show* and National Public Radio, in the *New York Times,* and in *Wired* and *Time* magazines.

She currently serves on the National Smart Growth Council, the Kyoto Cities Initiative International Advisory Council, and the Boston Mayor's Wireless Task Force.

Clayton Christensen is the Robert and Jane Cizik Professor of Business Administration at the Harvard Business School, with a joint appointment in the Technology and Operations Management and General Management faculty groups. His research and teaching interests center on managing innovation and creating new growth markets. He has been a faculty member since 1992.

A seasoned entrepreneur, Professor Christensen has founded three successful companies. The first, CPS Corporation, is an advanced materials manufacturing company that he founded in 1984 with several MIT professors. The second, Innosight, is a consulting and training company focused on problems of strategy, innovation, and growth that Christensen founded with several of his former students in 2000. Innosight Capital, the third firm, was launched in 2005. From 1979 to 1984, he worked

About the Contributors

with The Boston Consulting Group (BCG). In 1982 Professor Christensen was named a White House Fellow, and he served as assistant to U.S. Transportation Secretaries Drew Lewis and Elizabeth Dole.

Professor Christensen holds a BA with highest honors in economics from Brigham Young University and an MPhil in applied econometrics and the economics of less-developed countries from Oxford University, where he studied as a Rhodes Scholar. He received an MBA with high distinction from the Harvard Business School, graduating as a George F. Baker Scholar. He was awarded his DBA from the Harvard Business School in 1992.

Professor Christensen is the author or coauthor of several books, and his writings have won a number of awards.

Anders Dahlvig is the Group President and CEO of IKEA Services, a leading international retailer of home furnishing products.

Mr. Dahlvig joined IKEA Group in 1984. Since then he has held several positions, including Store Manager; Country Manager of United Kingdom; and Vice President, Europe. He assumed his current position in 1999 and has received various recognitions for IKEA Group's work to promote diversity.

In addition Mr. Dahlvig is a member of European Retail Round Table. In 2002 he received the Swedish award for Good Environmental Leadership for his independent and persistent work with environmental and sustainability issues, and in 2006 he received the U.S. Foreign Policy Association's Global Social Responsibility award.

Amelia Fawcett is Chairman of Pensions First, LLP, a financial services company launched in 2007 that aims to use the capital markets to tackle risks in U.K. final salary pension schemes.

Ms. Fawcett, a dual citizen of the United States and the United Kingdom, is the former Vice Chairman and COO of Morgan Stanley International. She had been with Morgan Stanley for twenty years, first joining the London office in 1987. She was then appointed Vice President in 1990, and Executive Director in 1992, moving up to the role of Managing Director and Chief Administrative Officer for the European operations in 1996.

In 2002 she was appointed Vice Chairman of Morgan Stanley International, responsible for development and implementation of the company's business strategy. She left her position in September 2006.

Ms. Fawcett is Chairman of the National Portrait Gallery's Development Board, Chairman of the London International Festival of Theater, and a Director of State Street Corporation.

Ken Freeman is Managing Director of the private equity firm KKR (Kohlberg Kravis Roberts & Co.)

and the former Chairman and CEO of Quest Diagnostics.

Mr. Freeman started his career at specialty glass and ceramics manufacturer Corning Incorporated, progressing through the financial function to lead several business turnarounds. In 1996 Quest Diagnostics, the health-care services company, was spun off from Corning.

Following his nine-year tenure at Quest Diagnostics, Mr. Freeman joined KKR as its Managing Director in May 2005. In this role he works closely with KKR's health-care team and other industry groups to source new investment opportunities and provide operational counsel and management expertise.

William Johnson is the Chairman, President, and CEO of the H.J. Heinz Company, the most global of all U.S.-based food companies.

Mr. Johnson joined Heinz in 1982 as General Manager—New Businesses for Heinz USA. In 1984 he was promoted to Vice President—Marketing for Ketchup, Foodservice, and Sauces. He was named President and CEO of Heinz Pet Products in 1988 and assumed leadership of Star-Kist Foods, Inc., in May 1992, when the pet food business and Star-Kist Seafood, a sister Heinz affiliate, re-merged.

In 1993 Mr. Johnson was named Senior Vice President of Heinz and joined the company's board of directors. His responsibilities included Heinz operations in the Asia/Pacific area, including

About the Contributors

Australia, New Zealand, China, Thailand, and South Korea, in addition to the canned tuna and pet food businesses of Star-Kist Foods, Inc. Mr. Johnson became President and Chief Operating Officer of Heinz in June 1996 and assumed the position of President and Chief Executive Officer in April 1998. He was named Chairman, President, and Chief Executive Officer in September 2000.

Prior to joining Heinz, Mr. Johnson was employed with Drackett, Ralston Purina, and Anderson-Clayton.

Mr. Johnson is a member of Emerson's board of directors where he serves on the board's compensation committee. He is a Director of the Grocery Manufacturers of America and the shipping company UPS. Mr. Johnson is also an active member of the University of Texas McCombs School of Business advisory council.

J. W. Marriott Jr. is Chairman and CEO of Marriott International, Inc., one of the world's largest lodging companies. His leadership spans more than fifty years, and he has taken Marriott from a family restaurant business to a global lodging company with more than twenty-eight hundred properties in sixty-eight countries and territories.

During high school and college, Mr. Marriott was employed by the Hot Shoppes restaurant chain, where he worked in a variety of positions.

He joined Marriott full-time in 1956 and soon afterward took over management of the company's

About the Contributors

first hotel. Mr. Marriott became Executive Vice President of the company and then, in 1964, became its President. He was elected CEO in 1972 and Chairman in 1985.

Mr. Marriott serves on the boards of Sunrise Assisted Living and the National Urban League and is Director of the Naval Academy Endowment Trust and the National Geographic Society. He is a member of the U.S. Travel and Tourism Promotional Advisory Board, the World Travel & Tourism Council, and the National Business Council.

He also chairs the President's Export Council and the Leadership Council of the Laura Bush Foundation for America's Libraries.

Richard Pascale is an Associate Fellow of Saïd Business School at Oxford University. He is also the Principal of Pascale & Brown.

Mr. Pascale spent twenty years as a member of the faculty at Stanford's Graduate School of Business, where he taught a course on organizational survival.

During his career he has also been a White House Fellow, Special Assistant to the Secretary of Labor, and senior staff on a White House Task Force. Mr. Pascale is an architect of corporate transformation programs and serves as an adviser to top management for a number of Fortune 100 companies.

Mr. Pascale is also an accomplished author.

About the Contributors

Giam Swiegers is CEO of Deloitte Australia, which is a member of Deloitte Touche Tohmatsu, one of the world's leading professional services organizations.

Mr. Swiegers began his career as an auditor with Deloitte in South Africa. Since then has worked for Deloitte on three continents and six cities. He moved into his current position in June 2003.

Since late 2007 Mr. Swiegers has been a member of Deloitte's Global Board and Global Board Governance Committee. He is also a member of the Deloitte Asia Pacific Executive Committee and the Global Innovation Council.

His stewardship of the Australian practice has led the firm to achieve the 2005 BRW/St. George Client Service award as the "Most Innovative Firm" in professional services in Australia, the 2006 *CFO* magazine "Accounting Services Firm" of the year award, and the 2008 Deloitte Global "Standard of Excellence Award" for innovation management.

On the people side, Mr. Swiegers has introduced an "inspiring women" initiative in the firm. For the sixth year running, Deloitte has been recognized as an employer of choice for women by the Equal Opportunity for Women Awards in 2007. Mr. Swiegers was awarded "2005 best CEO for the advancement of women in business." In September 2006 Mr. Swiegers was recognized by the Australian HR Awards, winning the "HR Champion—CEO" award.

⚔ ACKNOWLEDGMENTS ⚕

First and foremost, a heartfelt thanks goes to all of the executives who have candidly shared their hard-won experience and battle-tested insights for the *Lessons Learned* series.

Secondly, a special thanks to Mark Thompson for helping us frame the issues in a thoughtful and provocative Foreword, and for his continued involvement with 50 Lessons.

We would like to thank IBM for permission to use the Anders Dahlvig lesson, which was produced in partnership as part of a series inspired by the IBM Global CEO Study "The Enterprise of the Future." For more information on IBM's market leading series of C-suite Studies, please visit www.ibm.com/gbs/cxo.

Angelia Herrin at Harvard Business Publishing consistently offered unwavering support, good humor, and counsel from the inception of this ambitious project.

Brian Surette and David Goehring provided invaluable editorial direction, perspective and encouragement, particularly for this second series. Many thanks to the entire HBP team of designers, copy editors, and marketing professionals who helped bring this series to life.

Acknowledgments

Much appreciation goes to Jennifer Lynn and Christopher Benoît for research and diligent attention to detail, and to Roberto de Vicq de Cumptich for his imaginative cover designs.

Finally, thanks to our fellow cofounder James MacKinnon and the entire 50 Lessons team for the tremendous amount of time, effort, and steadfast support of this project.

—Adam Sodowick & Andy Hasoon
Directors and Cofounders, 50 Lessons

THE LAST PAGE IS ONLY THE BEGINNING

Watch Free *Lessons Learned*
Video Interviews and Get Additional Resources

You've just read first-hand accounts from the business
world's top leaders, but the learning doesn't have to
end there. 50 Lessons gives you access to:

**Exclusive videos featuring the leaders
profiled in this book**

**Practical advice for putting their
insights into action**

**Challenging questions that
extend your learning**

FREE ONLINE AT:
www.50lessons.com/crisis